Platypus Milk

Essays About Rome, Farming, And My Mother, Etc.

By

Jessica Harman

ISBN: 978-1-300-69006-1

Four-Forty-Four Press

Boston, Massachusetts

Platypus Milk

Essays About Rome, Farming, And My Mother, Etc.

Table of Contents

1

Rome Calling

It's the end of my days in Boston. You always know when it's the end of something. The icicles don't look attached to roofs, birds fly at your head, the sun looks blind. It seems like the regular world, but a little off. People on the subway begin being extra rude to you.

I've always believed that I can just pick a place, any place, and go there. There are certain places that call me; Rome, lately.

*

I walked past the Boston Public Library today, and the wind ruffled a giant plastic banner attached to the front of the building. The banner said something about sports heroes. I wasn't interested, and my non-interest in a headlining event—was it an event or what was it?—disturbed me. I was just not curious about this place that left me hollow inside, but I felt guilty for wanting to leave, too. I felt pushed and pulled by Boston, as if I should fall on my knees and praise the ground in the city where I finally found a doctor to help me with my illness (no one at home had been able to really help it, though Dr. Lefort had been able to stabilize it with his chalky-tasting pills and lithium that made me dizzy).

When you are being pushed out of a place by the laraes, those ancient spirits that preside over a place, you need another place to call you. Not all places call someone equally. Detecting which places are calling you is a process that unfolds over time, and it involves one's patience with one's human limitations as well as how the universal vibes communicate with us.

I first learned that Rome was calling me last night. While doing research into Paris, my sidebar on my computer screen kept giving me ads for Rome, advertising deals for hotels and airfares in February. I thought to myself, "Why do I have to go to Paris? It's so expensive, and besides, I'm fat and wouldn't be able to fit into anything anyone sold there. Why can't I go to Rome instead?" When I thought this, a waterfall appeared in my mind, splashing all over me. I felt so cool and free. I felt the word "yes" hiss through my body. I began imagining my life in Rome among all those ruins, fountains.

*

I remember seeing a movie, "Eat, Love, Pray," and there was a scene in Rome. The main character was eating dinner at an outside table at a restaurant with some friends, and the friends told her that there was one word that defined Rome. "Sex." The word itself does not entice me. The concept that a city can have one word that encapsulates it does entice me, however. It's a problem about how language relates to the world. I have to see a city that can be described as "Sex." I have to see a city that can be summed up in one syllable.

*

I know that some cities have colors. Paris and New York are blue. New York is ultramarine blue. I am uncertain about Paris because I have never been there. I imagine Paris blue more like water or sky, though.

Montreal is maroon.

Boston is gray-green.

To get to know a city's color, you look at the colors the weather brings to it; you let the streets move through you and find their dead ends in your blood vessels, spleen, and heart. You dream of the city and the color you dream is its true light.

I place great importance on the color of a city; it is the color of the poems I will write there.

*

I like Boston's gray-green. It's a very intellectual color, but there's not a lot of reminders of infinity and infinity's inherent beauty here; for that type of infinite clarity you need blue's crystalline aspects. The lack of blue makes me unhappy here. I need a blue place. Which does not explain why I am called to Rome, which I don't think is blue, if I am allowed to go out on a whim and take a wild guess.

I wonder what color Rome is. If its word is "Sex," then it's probably red, for passion. I do not know if I could live for a long time in a red city, but I'd like to taste it for a little while.

*

Whenever I am spending my last vestiges of time in a city, I begin doing a lot of walking, mostly because there's nothing else for me to do. I am now disengaged. I don't work. I don't volunteer. I simply exist. The parks with their pastiche of January-brown grass under the snow soak me up as I spill along pathways, downtown.

Sometimes I walk to the Starbucks opposite the Boston Public Library, and I sit on a maroon velvet chair and read my Kindle among the company of strangers.

I like being surrounded by strangers. Possibilities are endless. Anyone might talk to you at any point, bothering you, wanting to kiss you, or just ask you where you are from.

So far in the Starbucks this has happened on several occasions. Sometimes people with pockmarked faces who smell of cigarillos talk to me. Other times, I talk to them. No one has stuck, but it passes the time. I worry about myself when I talk to strangers to pass the time, since it means I am not feeling vulnerable enough in life. You need to feel vulnerable to be happy, and you need to feel that you have something to lose, and something someone could take away. Now, I'm at rock-bottom. It's a weird predicament: having everything, I have nothing.

Whenever I feel like I am stable and good and clean, I want to pick up a suitcase a fly away. I love living in a tentative situation. I like adventure and new things. Who doesn't?

I don't have to go to Rome. Even if I left Boston, I could go back to Montreal (which I probably will eventually do), but I need to fly around the world a few times first.

*

I love talking about where I am from, probably because I'm from an interesting place: Montreal. If I were from Des Moines, I'm not sure I'd feel the same way about boasting.

Everyone has a Montreal story in Boston, it seems, like the time they got really drunk in December and lay in the snow without a coat, or the time they almost got stabbed, or the time they got picked up by someone who wanted to teach them voodoo and they ended up smoking with him until dawn in his basement while he played ukulele and taught them folksongs. I have survived nights like that, too, when I was smashed and making snow angels in my long johns, before the night really got going.

I can smile and laugh when other people tell me about their strange need to get nearly naked when it's twenty degrees below zero outside, and the stars are hard little icy eyeballs above you, and the whole universe is watching, laughing, for no reason at all, other than that's what the universe does because existence is weird.

*

What will the stars look like in Rome? Will they sweat a little more in the heat and history of the Italian sun? I don't know, but I hope to one day know. Now, all I need is courage to take the leap, go to the embassy, learn some more Italian other than "birra," (the word for "beer,"), and start saving for the plane ticket over there. I can trust myself, though, because once I get an idea in my head, I follow through.

It's Rome or bust.

2

The Story My Mother Wants To Write

My Mom wants to write a story.

As a writer of stories myself, I sympathize with her. I know what an unwritten story feels like. It's a physical sensation, as if there's a comet (which is an asteroid on fire!) in your chest, trying to get out. It can't get out until you start writing the story.

Stories are dangerous things. They let things loose: gases, flames, orbits in hitherto unexplored regions of space.

A story, once written, changes things. It changes everything. Your dream has become real, and in its youth, like something just born, it is both vulnerable as well as needy. Like a baby, it will keep you up at night with its crying. A story is not a safe, neat thing. Like anything that belongs to the heart, it is messy. It splatters its food everywhere, so that when it eats (you must feed the story) mashed potatoes and baby-food peas get on the linoleum and walls.

The worst thing about a story, though, is not how it disturbs your life and causes ripples on the pond; what is scariest is how much you love that story you wrote, as if it were your own flesh, part of your own family lineage of chromosomes. This new love upsets everything. For one thing, it takes away from the loved you already have. Your story begins to come between you and your husband, wife, boyfriend, or girlfriend. Your story demands that you choose it as number one. The worst thing about this demand is that if you choose your story over a human love, which all good writers must, you now love something that is unhuman. This poses some obvious problems. Stories do not love you back. You give and give, and they take and take; that is how it worls.

Stories have to do with being human, but they are not human beings, and cannot replace them. If you love your story over love between human beings, you are a real writer, but you're also a lost soul, in many ways. You give up the happiness of the feel of flesh. Your new salvation is the feel of a pen in your hands or the gliding of your fingers over a computer keyboard. It's a sad state of affairs, some would say, but the writers of stories feel something: they are creating something that might be a work of truth, for others. More people share your story than your relationship. You are closing down in one way, but opening up in others.

I think this change is not something my Mom is unaware of. She doesn't want to upset the apple cart. She likes the way things in her life are. She doesn't want to move her heart to the iceberg where writers live, alone and afloat in the Arctic sea of words.

She has a story, though, and it is in her, and she wants to tell it, one day. There is no law that says she can't. There are also no guarantees that she will. Some people never tell their stories. I hope she tells her story, though, because I want to hear it. I try to encourage her, though I know how much work it takes from conception to completion. Years, mountain ranges appear and disappear, geography that otherwise would have been ordinary days happens. There are snow storms in June instead of sunny weather. You inflict the writer's life upon yourself, even for just one measly story, which might be nothing, or might be everything. You just don't know until you write it. Then you know just what power you have, what joy words have in them, what universes you have spinning inside you.

*

I love to write. I decided I wanted to be a writer at an early age, so I've been practicing for a while (I'm thirty-eight now, that gives me thirty years of practice). My first story was about a conversation between a raisin and a tomato who decided to escape the kitchen. I hope I have come a long way since then, escaping many of my own proverbial kitchens (I never liked to cook).

I wonder how my Mom feels at having given birth to a writer who has not yet made it, or hit the big time. I publish in small magazines, and sometimes in big journals, where my name gets lost alongside the larger headliners.

I know my Mom wants me to be happy, just as I want her to be happy. I know I wouldn't be happy if I didn't give birth to stories, if I didn't let my fireworks spin out into realities of paragraphs. I need to make metaphors, to say what love is. I believe all stories are love stories, of sorts. Love is a bagel, a throw pillow, a beautiful waterfall. Love is a walk across a lake while not knowing if it is completely frozen or not.

Other people are so tentative. When you're a non-writer, you want that ice of love to be solid. You don't want to fall in the lake and get wet, but when you're love is the love of writing, and your lover is a story, you want that ice to break. You want to get underneath the surface, since writing is about seeing the invisible under the surfaces that so often appear frozen.

*

When you begin to write, you start making the commitment to see what's beneath the surface. What does the light falling across her face that way really mean? It's a cloudy day on the day of my math exam; what is the secret meaning behind that? You can't just go along with things anymore. You have to investigate them. You're a detective of the human mind and the heart and the world. You see everything, forgive nothing at times, while at the other times forgiving everything with infinite compassion. So while it's easy to want to be a writer, it's not easy to make that commitment when you begin seeing what it involves. Yet some still choose it.

I am a writer because I have nothing else to be. I was called. I don't care what happens. I am committed, already, and my boyfriend knows this; he is second to my thesaurus.

It might make him sad, but as a writer, I have to be a little heartless.

*

Writers are sometimes not the nicest, cleanest, neatest people (though some of them may be. I know a few who manage to be really good people, though I am struggling). My apartment is full of dirty dishes breeding fruit flies. My sheets need to be washed. My furniture is the kind that is purchased at church rummage sales when they clean out the school supply closet (some sturdy folding chairs, for example, grace my kitchen). But I am happy. I am a writer.

*

I want my mother to write her story, because writing is a happy thing, in the same way that scaling a glacier or climbing Mount Everest is fun. The torture is the amazing part about it; the fact that you did it is amazing. It was there, and it was there to be done, and so it was done, all with uncertain footsteps placed one at a time on the face of a cliff. It is the ultimate thing.

*

My Mom won't tell me what her story is. She says she doesn't want to tell anyone, until she writes it. I want to hear the story, so I encourage her to write the first sentence. It won't look like anything on its own, I tell her. You have to write a few paragraphs, set it aside for a day or two, then write another few paragraphs, until you have ten pages. Once you have ten pages, you have something: a rough draft. As one writer said, "There are no great writers, only great rewriters." Now that you have a rough draft, you can rewrite your story, put in metaphors where there were none before, write scenes between the scenes that are already there. You can begin concentrating on craft. You can take things out, put things in. But you've done it. You've begun to tell your story.

3

The Farm

I never know how people are going to react when I tell them about the farm. Once, I told my friend Sendra, as we munched a ketchup-drowned plate of fries in Montreal's Hard Rock Café (which was as deserted as a desert with no dessert, apparently not the place to be, which is why we were there; we liked to go where there was no one else but us).

She said, "Oh wow, a farm, you mean with chickens and cows and everything?"

I said, "Yup."

I knew she was trying to get rid of me in those days, but she was one of my few friends, so I clung like Saran Wrap to cold oatmeal. She was learning Italian, and going on to bigger and better things. She was moving to Europe with her film-maker boyfriend. I was full of America at that point, though exactly what about America I don't remember, except that I kept telling people that America takes who you are, and multiplies it by ten. I still believe that's true. American culture allows you to be who you are, and no one else. That is its virtue and its torture; I live in America, now (Boston, Massachusetts), and America magnifies my personality mercilessly. It's heaven and hell at the same time. That's what America does to you: it makes your life both heaven and hell at once. Human beings are paradoxes, and America will bring this into focus so sharply you'll think you're staring at your soul in the mirror when really it's just your regular face.

There is an inevitable pain to life, both physical and spiritual. Cultures deal with this discomfort in different ways. America deals with it the fat way. Canada (and the farm I am talking about in Canada) deals with it in the Canadian way. I don't know what that is; it's been a while since I've lived there long enough to have an understanding of the place. I forget easily. I just remember it was unbearably cold, making the pain of life sharper, but crisper and more refreshing, since the snowfall lent an invigorating beauty to the place. Also, people encourage each other to stare at the falling snow and glean its aesthetic, there, which I have noticed isn't so much the case here in America.

The farm is about an hour and a half drive from Montreal, in the Eastern Townships of Quebec. There are two cows, six pigs, ten chickens, and a horse named Mulberry. There's also a mule named Ralph, a cat named

Chico, and two dogs named Zeus and Cody. The dogs have mismatching eyes, so they look like David Bowie (both of them. They're brothers).

There's a garden that yields the best corn on Earth. (The Snapple ad campaign lies. The best stuff on Earth is not Snapple, but the corn from my aunt's farm's garden.) My aunt also grows tomatoes, beans, snap peas, radishes, carrots, spices like basil and parsley, and daisies for her bees to become fat with pollen for her bee-keeping practice.

She made the wooden hives for her bees herself. She had to measure wood to an eighth of an inch precision. I do not understand her patience with craftsmanship, but she likes woodworking and fixing things, making, sewing, and baking things. She likes tending flowers, gardens, animals, and people. This is why she lives on a farm.

The farm is not hers. Technically, it is her boyfriend's and his ex-wife's and her father's. They all built the farmhouse, sheds, barns, and coops in the sixties. They built everything by hand, and now after broken marriages and broken hearts, no one who originally had to do with the farm wants to leave it, so they all live there. Farm politics can get hairy, so I keep out of it. I'm just there to visit my aunt, feed some chickens, and eat some corn.

I like my aunt. She is my favorite relative other than my parents and stepfather. Scrabble is her favorite game. She has good choice in movies. Last time I was there, we watched "Iris," a movie about Iris Murdoch getting Alzheimer's. It doesn't sound that good, but I learned a lesson I needed to learn, and that is that a relationship takes one exciting person to lead and one sweet person to follow. I am an exciting leader-type, so that justifies my relationship with one of my ex-boyfriends whom I'm still very good friends with, Eric. If I lead, he can follow. The film also gave me the image of Kate Winslet on a bicycle looking free and happy, and I brought away something from that as an aesthetic moment.

*

When I told Eric about the farm, he wanted to go. My aunt's knowledge of kung fu lured him. He wanted to learn how to kick some ass in a peaceful rural setting. The contrast excited him. Despite the fact that my aunt hasn't competed in a kung fu competition in twenty years did not deter him. I informed him that even though she was out of practice, she might be persuaded to show him the basics among the blueberry bushes.

The farm is a bastion of toughness. Kung fu is just the beginning.

You have to have a certain dispassionate outlook to tend animals that are going to be slaughtered by people you actually talk to. It's not as in city life where pork and chicken come packaged in a cold, clean meat section, so that you only have to imagine the cruelty those animals endured as the scenarios flash briefly in your mind before you tuck them back safely into your subconscious. On the farm, you love the animals. You see them every day. And then, one day, you kill them. Still, when the meat comes out of the oven and you're waiting hungrily at the table, you're glad that you sacrificed little Cindy the chicken, who had been your trusting friend throughout the summer. It's all so brutal and heartless. Like most things brutal and heartless, there is a perverted joy in it.

I told Eric, a vegetarian, that we did slaughter animals on the farm, when he asked if we did.

"I don't want any animal to be slaughtered on my account," he said. "I wouldn't be able to handle it."

"Don't worry about it. The farm's kind of weird, anyway."

That's how our conversation about the farm ended.

*

Sitting on a handmade bench and watching the sun go down like honey dripping on the hills of the Eastern Townships, a warm cup of after-dinner coffee in your hands, makes you feel really at peace. That's what it's like to sit on the verandah of the farm, which wraps around the farmhouse.

There is an artistic aesthetic to the farm. I will call it, "Rustic surrealism." From the beams of the verandah hang various objects with curious shapes: old tools, things made out of clay, things made of nails stuck into clay. They aren't supposed to be anything in particular. They're supposed to be enjoyed for the silhouettes they cast, much like abstract art and its shapes. We know this on the farm: that the farm has a hidden genius to it. This genius is a type of art of living. It's the shapes of the objects hanging from the roof of the verandah, it's the photographs framed in the house of Alberta panoramas juxtaposed with Saskatchewan panoramas so a part of Canada is spiced together, it's the photographs in the living room of snow sculptures the kids made when they were young; it's even the flavor of the honey and the pie recipe I invented for apple coconut tart (the one and only). The genius is the goodness of the quirky look and taste and smell of life on the farm. You have to love it.

I wanted to share the genius of the farm with Eric, even though part of me thinks the genius of the farm is diseased. It's beautiful, but sometimes it's a little too surreal for me. This absurdity strikes me as particularly Quebecois, or at least foreign to an American aesthetic, where everything is so practical. Yet given the choice of whether to live on any old farm or a surrealist farm, I'd choose to be on a surrealist farm in a second. There are interesting tensions, there. There is a striving to make life into art. There is the knowledge that human life needs things to decipher that lend themselves to a deep code. It's not all about chickens and pigs.

*

I am both an American and Canadian citizen. I live in America, now, about six hours drive from the farm if you drive as the crow flies.

Boston is a classy city, even though I live in a sort of suburb of mixing social classes, so that Harvard professors live next to part-time landscapers, and lawyers live in big houses next to small houses where drug addicts live.

Despite the weirdness of my location, I care what people think, here. Besides, I am beginning to think that everywhere on Earth is weird where there are people, so I'm becoming less judgmental.

Once, when I was coming back from the farm, I was carrying a plastic bag with handles made from an improvised twist of ropes. It was so embarrassing to walk through the city with my rope-handle plastic bag. My bag screamed, "I'm a hick!" I was not pleased.

When I got home, I was so relieved that my roommates didn't see me with my farm-made bag. My aunt and her boyfriend had been mighty proud of their making of the bag from things they had lying around. It was just so darned useful.

Being useful and making useful things is very valued on the farm. It's not all surrealist art. You still have to feed the chickens, pluck eggs out from under hens, and make a bag out of rope lying around on the verandah. You have to know what to do to make things work and keep things going.

*

Sometimes the inhabitants of the farm wonder who they would be if they lived in the city, I know. But talking to my cousins there, I suppose they are happy. They have a whole world to themselves. They have art and eggs, surrealism and milk, beauty and blueberries. They have everything in a perfect balance.

*

My father is from Kansas City. He's never been to my aunt's farm. Now, he lives in a hospital in New York City, and thinks about things as the snow falls gently outside his window. He says he thinks about his life in Canada, and how tough a town Montreal is. Montreal is a tough town for Americans. They are disliked, and sometimes stabbed while on vacation if too loud and obnoxious, so the urban legends go. The college kids come up to drink beer at an earlier age than they are allowed to in Vermont and Massachusetts; the Quebec legal drinking age is eighteen, instead of twenty-one.

When I lived in Montreal, every summer the tourists would flood St. Catherine Street, and they would be loud in their loud clothing, too. I disliked them. I had not yet experienced Boston, where I'd learn that red shorts were considered cheerful and colorful and brave, instead of just in ridiculously bad taste. The aesthetics of the countries are so different, even though the armies usually fight on the same side in a war.

Montreal people dress in dark, tasteful clothing, not pink shirts paired with red shorts.

We smoke our cigarettes slowly over coffee.

We believe in silk. We believe there are things that are wonderful that are not practical, such as the patterns of bird flight, the way snow falls, the zigzags of frost on a window.

I know certain Americans who believe in these things, too, but they are often considered silly, or wishers on superfluous things. Yet they have a good aesthetic, in my opinion, because it's the superfluous things that draw us into deeper meaning, deeper beauty.

*

Stereotypes are not good, but I have been looked on as a silly dreamer enough here in Boston, so that now I'm bitter. I long for Montreal, but then I think of the long winter, and I shudder. That is one thing I can't say I miss.

My father was very surprised by Canadian winters when he escaped Kansas, dodging the draft for the Vietnam War because, in his words, he "didn't want to kill anybody."

"But Dad, maybe they would kill you first." I said.

He said, "No, I don't think so."

He was a college football star. No one was going to kill him. But Montreal brought him to his knees, weeping, eventually, in a rooming house off of a side street in lower

Westmount, where the social classes mixed, where sometimes prostitutes wandered the streets.

He was a strong, practical, intelligent man, and this does not go over well in Montreal, where whimsy rules, where weakness and poverty are seen as virtues in God's eyes. Sometimes it amazes me how much Montreal and America have opposite views of the same thing. Take a hole in one of my sweaters, for example. Now that I live in America, I think that I need to buy a new sweater when I get a hole in it. In Montreal, however, I'd pick at the loose thread, make the hole a little larger, because holes in your clothes meant you were poor and a bit closer to the virtues that God valued.

I love both countries. I love both ways. I wish I could have everything in one place, but it's impossible, because things need to add up to a whole, and too many contradictions can't exist. In any one place, look at the tensions that hold it together. Sometimes I wonder why there are such big paradoxes in people's behavior, yet still you cannot have everything, everywhere.

*

I would like to show my father the farm, and have him understand it. It's a part of me that's very un-American, but still really cool. The farm has become a part of me because my aunt is there, and I love her. We play Scrabble on the internet constantly, and whenever she makes a word, like "Fox," "Horse," "Pig," or "Radish," I think of where she is sitting at her computer, the big picture window looking out on what is a frozen, snow-covered garden.

4

Ants

Talya's house was the house I wanted to live in. It was so square, and had two floors. The address was in oversized numbers next to the door, which was illuminated by a large circular, flat light: a disc like the moon, but made of plastic, attached to the brick so that it looked like it was hovering. I would go over to her house at night, sometimes, fighting my way through clouds of gnats that like to swarm in Northern city summers. Gnats are attracted to me more so than other people, I have found, and it's the same thing with mosquitoes. I suppose I like insects more than most people, though, so the feeling is mutual. I rejoice when a good luck ladybug lands on my forearm, for example, and I really don't mind spiders at all, because they're good luck, too. Talya didn't like insects. She hated them. Once, she spent a whole afternoon squishing ants by stomping on them while wearing her new sneakers. But she said the ants got their revenge. The next day, there were three times as many swarming the cracking concrete porch. Ants were pouring out of the cracks in the concrete, she said, and then she showed me. There were thousands, perhaps millions of ants making rivers of squiggling black along her porch. She was afraid, and that's when the ants started to come into the house. Talya would take a clean glass from the cupboard, only to find a couple of little six-legged friends on it.

5

The Overly Critical People's Club

The living room and kitchen in our place in Brookline were beige. It was safer this way. No one could disagree on beige, we thought, so Val went ahead and bought the hide-a-bed and □apas an in the neutral spectrum. We even had a concrete squirrel that was beige, and we put it next to the fake wood TV stand which, like the rug, was beige. It was all very boring, but it gave one the sense that people of good sense lived here, which was true, if you judged by my roommates.

I was crazy, but like all people who know they're crazy, I was a little less crazy than most crazy people who don't know they're crazy. It was still wonderfully boring in that house despite my craziness, and we were happy. Maria made her tea in an artistic tea ceremony that she insisted was particularly Russian; it had to do, she said, with the timing of when you drop the lemon slice into your cup. A certain amount of time had to elapse from boiling point of the water to lemon-slice interaction.

The tea was a part of us all, now. We drank Maria's tea at midnight when we were all awake, discussing our boring lives. Sometimes we played chess. We formed an impromptu secret society we called "The Overly Critical People's Club," in which we could bitch about trivial matters that annoyed us to no end during our workaday lives in Boston. Women with strollers and old women with walkers were among our favorite pet peeves. People who talk about horses too much, subway drivers who closed the doors on your before you were in, people who thought that America was the opposite of France. We were still young enough then to not understand the foibles of the very young and very old: we had to care for no one but ourselves, and besides, we were spry and in our late-twenties, employed, talented, and pretty decent looking. We had no worries, really, except the possibility that our concepts of grandeur for our lives wouldn't work out in the end (would one of us please hurry up and finally get a poetry manuscript accepted by the Yale Younger Series of Poets?). But of course, everything would work out in the end, because we were us, and life had pretty much worked out up until this point, without our actually having to do any serious thinking or develop compassion.

One can be a poet without compassion, I realize, now, but it is always much better to be a poet with compassion. This was one major thing we would have to learn, and that Al would help me to learn. I have not mentioned Al yet. We will get to him.

We were poets with a pleasingly beige living room. What more could we ask?

Maria told me that the squirrel made of concrete was once on the set of a David Lynch film, and I believed her. I was star struck by the squirrel.

One day, our fourth roommate Larry (whom we had little to do with because he was always busy and felt the same way about us), told us he got a promotion at work, and had to move from the Boston area to New York City, but we shouldn't worry: a mutual friend of all of ours (sort of), Al ,wanted to move in.

Al.

Of course, I wanted Al to move in. He was Maria's hot friend (just a friend), and he was a foodie (into wine and cheese, therefore he understood my French Canadian roots, I believed), and he liked our beigeness. He wanted a piece of that beigeness.

*

Val hedged and was uncertain about Al, but I said he could move in whenever the hell he wanted. I had only met him twice, and on both occasions he was at our house drinking tea and playing Scrabble with Maria. He seemed to be able to hold his own in a challenging Scrabble game: proof positive that he would make a good roommate, in my books.

As we sat at the kitchen table, which we didn't like to admit we had bought at Target, I said, "What, exactly, is your problem, Val?"

With a flip of her russet bangs over her apple-shaped freckled face, she declared, "Nothing. He can move in."

*

The nearest Starbucks, where Al worked, was a block away. I just had to cross one street. Every morning I would drag my sleepy, not-yet caffeinated body there. The walk was pleasant, along stately Beacon Street. There were brownstones, three stories or four stories high.

Once when Maria and I were taking a walk down to Coolidge Corner, the birthplace of JFK as well as a shopping area with a pretty good Trader Joe's, she said that she couldn't believe the brownstones were considered elegant when she first came over from Russia. They weren't ornate. To her, elegant and fancy were synonyms, but she would learn that to a Bostonian, elegant and fancy were opposites.

The brownstones were so plain. I thought of Montreal, and we didn't have many brownstones there, either. It wasn't a thing, there, like magenta or lavender spiraling staircases on aquamarine Victorian houses were.

I suppose most cultures consider ornate things pleasant, and plain things boring, and I don't know how Boston got to be the opposite. Everything was very bland, on Beacon Street particularly, because it was a bastion of English history. At least that's what it seemed to me, but I can enjoy any area that is considered rich because what's upscale makes my bones tingle in a wonderful way. There's the bad tingle and the good tingle, and expensive areas of town made me just simply tingle all over! I didn't want to be materialistic, and I wouldn't have admitted it to most people, but I was a material girl. I was lucky to live in Brookline, even though it was a little boring. Sometimes I really craved nothing else but a magenta spiraling staircase on an orange Victorian mansion with aquamarine turrets, like they have on *Le Plateau* in Montreal, where I am from.

As I walked to Starbucks, I anticipated a crumbly blueberry scone and a hot coffee. I like Pike Place, the medium blend, because I am a medium-anything kind of girl, just out of necessity, not out of nature. I can't usually afford extremes. There was also some philosophy behind my forcing myself to be moderate in all things; I remembered the teachings of Socrates. Don't super-size me: that's too American. And don't give me espresso in little cups like some euro-girl: I like my bang for my buck to take more time than just one gulp.

So I get my cup of *grande* Pike's Place every morning, and I have come to know Al from there, too. He is always a pleasant, shining face, but I like to keep him at a distance, even though (or since?) he is a friend of my friends. I'm weird that way.

*

I learned over a slow and painful process of hazing after moving here for work (I do medical research on diet and exercise part time when I am not writing poetry in my free time), that Americans want to know the practical application of everything. If you talk about God, they want to know what your beliefs can *do.* Everything has to be plugged into the wall and giving off a certain amount of heat or light. I suppose that's okay, but it didn't leave room for the things I cherish best of all: pointless poems written on bathroom walls in train stations, stained glass that was done with a tenderness beyond love, elaborate flower gardens with twenty-five different kinds of tulips for no reason at all, antiques, costume jewelry, funny socks, expensive throw pillows (those especially make my left ventricle tingle), eating cheese as if it were an art. Call me a snob who is into an elitist aesthetic as opposed to a pristine utilitarianism, but I like what's simply beautiful and has no other use at all other than to shine.

However, even though I have champagne taste, I have a beer wallet. But I get my kicks.

*

One day when Al saw me at Starbucks, he greeted me exuberantly, and gave me a free coffee.

"It would be awesome if you lived with us," I said.

He had dimples underneath his five-o'clock-shadow at nine o'clock in the morning. I knew some things about Al: he wrote poetry, too, and he liked food, and his uncle Orvis owned a vineyard in Napa, California, and he was originally from Pittsburgh, and he liked the author Michael Chabon, too.

"Maria said I could." His smile brightened the room.

"Oh, cool," I said, happy, but taken aback that Val had actually given Maria the go-ahead. "That'll be in two weeks."

"Yeah."

"You'll be so near your work." I said, making conversation.

He said, "Yeah, it's cool." Because there was a fat man wearing three scarves in September behind me, I moved on, taking my coffee over to the table where you can add your own cream and sugar. "See you later."

I smiled, knowing I don't have a pretty smile, but what can you do if you don't have a pretty smile when you smile? You don't flash it for too long. Just a quickness in your face, then you turn away, hoping you have not horrified anyone for too long. This is how I've come to deal with not having a pretty smile. I do have a pretty face, even though I'm chubby.

You can't be all pretty. There's got to be something about you that's God-awful, because you're human.

I wondered if Al would make a good roommate, and I was suddenly uncertain, and startled that I had not really considered the question seriously before agreeing, but it was all done and agreed upon. I turned around and waved before leaving Starbucks, and even though he was serving a lady in a fur coat who had a toy poodle in her bag, he caught my eye as he spilled some change into her extended hand.

Al.

I thought it would all be okay.

We could now all sit around at midnight and be overly critical together. He probably had some stories about Starbucks! But I wasn't sure. Now that I gave it some thought, what irked me about Al was that he wanted to much to be liked. Something about that made me not respect him as much as I would have respected, for example, Larry, who didn't give a damn what you thought of him. This all worried me. Was I antisocial? Was it good to be liked and likeable, as Al certainly was?

*

He brought three bottles from Uncle Orvis' vineyard, with labels that said different crude things. One bottle of wine had a label decorated with flowers around the border that said, "Sexy Bitch Face," another said, "Matt, I'm Constipated," and another said, "Uncle Orvis's devil-fart brew." I was left speechless at the tastelessness of all this, as he showed me each bottle's label, laughing. I laughed, too, a fake sort of laughter at first, but then a real laugh, when I began seeing the joke-names were funny, if you looked at it a certain way. You had to think of real names, and contrast them. It was the contrast between high brow and low brow that was hilarious.

"Can I help you bring your stuff in?" I asked, looking at the U-Haul truck out the window, parked by the curb outside our building.

A friend of his named Mike came in and put a box and a fancy bronze wine rack on the kitchen table, then smiled as I imagined all of Al's friends did. He knew people-people, because he was a people-person with a nice smile. In fact, he looked pretty darned good-looking when he smiled. He was smiling then, in the kitchen, not for any other reason than that he was moving in, or alive, or something. I briefly wondered, as if a dragonfly were flitting into the tree-hole of my brain for just a flicker, if I could handle someone so good-natured in proximity to me for extended periods of time. Maybe it would change me. Maybe I would finally do something like take my mood stabilizers, which I hadn't been taking, as of late, which I knew was a mistake.

Wait a minute—I caught myself thinking (or even *feeling?*)—was Al's moving in making me want to be a better person? A small alarm went off in my mind, and it occurred to me that I was actually attracted to Al. I like to think of myself as the Ice Queen. I am attracted to no one. I don't let anyone melt my ice. Nope.

And Al, of all people? Al of the devil-fart wine, which he tenderly placed in the wine rack that he put on the corner of the counter? Al who might give me a sip of Sexy Bitch Face?

I wanted to say, "Wait, that's where I put my cornflakes," but decided against it, on account of it being potentially bossy, which I know I can be (I didn't like that about myself—another thing I wanted to change, and that Al was making me consider changing).

My question was still hanging there like a chad on a vote, and Al said kindly, to my relief, "Nah. We don't have that much to bring in. No need to help us. I know I have a lot of kitchen stuff, but that's about it." He put his hands on his hips in a posture my mother called, "The peasant's dance" when I was growing up, when she didn't want me to do it.

*

After that, whenever I went in or out of the house, I looked at our mailbox in the vestibule of the apartment building. The light bulb in the old, high ceiling flickered like a candle being blown by the wind. Time was so freaky and fleeting, and I was feeling myself as being vulnerable, in those days, for some reason.

I looked at Al Maller's name next to mine, Val's, and Maria's on the mailbox. He had written his name so tenderly in careful block letters. Al. Sometimes the letters would ripple and sparkle, and I knew it was because I wasn't taking my medication.

But I stopped there every day on my way out and way in, just to look at his name.

*

He was always frying pierogies while drinking a glass of red wine, Uncle Orvis' preferred vintage, apparently (I never saw him drinking white or rosé).

We didn't talk much the first week; I was skittish around him.

His girlfriend came over one night. When I went in to make some coffee in the electric coffee maker that I used when Starbucks was closed, Al asked me to illuminate a point he was trying to make about Robert Bly's light-filled translations as opposed to the darkness of his poetry. I said something vaguely intelligent while under the hellish red scrutiny of his girlfriend's gaze.

I interacted with Al about poetry for a few moments as my coffee brewed, feeling that I had him. I had him! I felt his girlfriend's jealousy, and it made me happy.

She said as my coffee machine was making burbling sounds, "I'm a musician. I play the saxophone. I don't know as much about poetry as you guys."

I was happy for Al that he had a girlfriend.

*

I only saw Al's big-boned girlfriend once, then I heard through the grapevine that they broke up. She had broken his heart, according to Maria.

I heard Maria and Al talking in the kitchen one day, and he said, "I'm throwing all the shit she gave me out. I want to be rid of it all. If she wants it back, tough shit."

That was the first time I had seen Al be mean or spiteful in any way. I chocked it up for future reference, though. I thought, "He's not all sweetness, smiles, and funny names for what has the fragrant bouquet of a pretty decent vintage wine."

It was that moment that things turned around.

One day, nevertheless, I decided to be normal and say hi to Al once again, in a way that wasn't just in passing and out of politeness.

I was wearing black, because I always do. It's my signature style.

He was in the kitchen frying pierogies.

"Hi, Al," I said.

"Hi," he said. We didn't mention his girlfriend, or coffee, or wine. "Want a pierogie?" He asked.

"Sure." I did. I love pierogies. They're so simple with their doughy coating, yet so comforting with their meaty center. I wanted comfort food, because I am always in a state of discomfort, and needing comfort. Such sweet, wholesome comfort! Too bad, I thought, that even the simplest things come with a twist that is the uncertainty that belongs to everything, and if they don't, there's probably something wrong.

We listened to the hissing of the pierogies frying in the pan, and for a moment, I was confused by my own happiness. It seemed so easy, all of a sudden. I didn't know if I'd be able to handle something that wasn't difficult.

I stared into the pattern of the kitchen table cloth—flowers. I did not understand, and I didn't know what I didn't understand.

All of a sudden, there was a pierogie before me.

"Want some sour cream?" He asked, getting a plastic tub of good stuff out of the fridge.

I wondered if Al could be persuaded to enjoy the Overly Critical People's Club. I wondered if he was one of us, or what it would take for me to become one of him.

6

My Weaknesses As A Teacher:

A Meditation On A Snowy Day

The pain was in the snow this morning, and I didn't know if I was a tiger or a spider plant. Being a human being seemed out of the question: too little money for a cup of coffee today of all mornings. Starbucks gleamed in the blizzard like a lighthouse out at sea, and that's when I changed into a ship. Water sloshed over my frozen starboard ribs, and I screamed inside. I didn't let any sound loose as I trudged in my Uugs down Brattle Street, appearing unaffected by the wind. I had not been knocked down or hit by a mad bicyclist—I was merely imagining the worst as the best was happening (often the situation with me). I was freaking out because my doctor had left a message saying my lab tests were abnormal, but I had not actually talked to her about that yet. I wanted to cy on my way to teach my English as a Second Language class, but I was silent, for the most part. Maybe a sigh hissed from my lips. It's hard to remember, now.

I was unhappy about going somewhere. Tin-colored ivy snaked around the winter sun. I wasn't in love with anything or anyone, and that seemed a little odd to me. I am always full of some type of romance, but today, I was not. I wanted to be dead. It just seemed easier.

I was going somewhere. I was taking the bus and then the subway to Wellington with its orange line signs and friendly neighborhood faces. Everett was such a neighborhood. The faces seemed familiar even though I'd never been there, before. I had learned that, yesterday, when I taught my first English as a Second Language class at a community center. I had never done that, before. I had never stood up there are said, "I am, You have, I want," so directly, as if there were nothing to it but memorization.

There is a structure under the structure, but that is called feeling, and you cannot teach it.

You cannot teach the desire to learn, but there the students all were, looking eagerly at me. I stood in front of a white board and wrote things next to little drawings of the sun and the rain. We were small talking about the weather, because they didn't know how, and I was teaching them to do that. I had visions of them at the grocery checkout counter, saying to the cashier, "Cold weather we're having today, isn't it?" It is not as simple as it looks. They kept saying "Thank-you" in out of place places in our mock situations, in which I was them, and they were supposed to be me. I said,

“Don’t say thank-you. It’s not necessary.” You do not thank someone for saying it’s been quite a rainy spring. It seemed funny to me, but somehow wonderfully formal.

It went well, yesterday. I felt loved. I felt like I learned something about Haiti, where they were all from. I wanted the students’ voodoo, their beaches, their wars, their search for life in a new land. They gave me all that in just a day, but that was yesterday. The serpent twined like branching ivy around the sun in my dreams, and the snow became blood, and I was re-born as a rabbit chased by the wolf-moon, but I won the race, and won the world.

But today I could not face them, again. I did not know why. Was it the snow? Was it the lack of coffee in my bloodstream? Was it my dumb fear of everything meaningful that might define me so that I am no longer just a floating cloud?

Halfway through the snow, I called Eric, the director of the school, and said I just couldn't do it. I had become ice inside. The world had at last got to me, and I was unable to give of myself without breaking down, cracking.

He said, "Feel better soon," and hung up without a goodbye.

*

I am at home after my adventures. I just came home and slept, and thought about my former students. Did they miss me? Was I loved, or was that merely part of their routine? What will become of all the heat in the world, going around, warming people up when they least suspect it? And what will happen to all this cold that gets in the heart and makes passion useless?

*

Inside me, I have Eden, and there is Eve, listening to the snake. I do not know what this has to do with anything, except that it explains a certain amount of fear that I feel. The fear has no other explanation. I shake sometimes just thinking about walking down School Street, which is in a very modest suburban area, and taking the bus. I have done this many times before. Nothing ever happens. But it's the fear that has got me with its bear trap claws around my ventricles. I am uneasy with the concept of love, too. I just don't want to be a shipwreck in somebody else's arms. I don't want to face you, or me, or anyone. The voices are talking about me. They aren't asking me any questions. The voices aren't there to listen to me—they're there to correct, criticizes, and fill the beautiful world with a terrible sea made of blood.

I take my medication, but it just masks the monster. The weather continues.

I was afraid, today, that I didn't have enough coffee in my veins to be awake. When I am asleep, I am more insane. If I don't have my coffee, I can't think like a human being. I didn't have coffee this morning because I ran out and couldn't afford anymore. I can get some more on Thursday. Until then , I'm sinking.

I know that there is, technically, great beauty in the world. We leave continents of time and space to go to new places, and then we see what it's like, there. It's always different. If we grew up in a red city, then we move to a blue one. Some people don't, but some people, like me, are innate travelers. We have to learn the new language of the place, its customs of acceptable eye contact. The codes we use keep me going. They fascinate me like Slinkies going down stairs. They are waterfalls of things that are not water. They move like grace itself.

*

I came here, to Massachusetts, eleven years ago. Boston was a place I'd never been to, before. I just picked a place on the map and went. That's the easiest thing to do.

The first thing that happened in my new city, as I walked out of the train station, was that someone in a truck for a landscaping company or something asked me for directions. I told him I had never been to Boston before, and that I just arrived two minutes ago. He was nonplussed, and drove away with a stubbly frown. I didn't yet know that he didn't need to know about me, as people in Montreal would have. I just needed to spew a formula that I had yet to learn, and say with a smile, "Sorry, I don't know where that is. I'm not from this area." No need to launch into my life story complete with shifty eyes, which my friends say is my very hilarious signature facial expression (I'll be saying something really banal but my eyes get all shifty. Little do they know what thoughts I am covering up with what boring things I let spew from my mouth).

I have learned a lot by being in Boston. I have learned about having a sense of community. Montreal is not so big on community. They're about coffee one-on-one. Cafés are always full of the coppery sheen of people talking. Things get done over cappuccino. I like that, but I also like the way an issue is probed in depth, often, to find out what it's true nature is, in a certain light that would catch prisms. In Montreal, people want to know what things are, just as they also do in Boston, but Bostonians are more forward-looking and practical than Montrealers. Montrealers want to know how one can heal the rift that runs through everything broken, and everything that is real is already broken in some way, they believe. Only unreal things are perfect. They do not pretend as if it were otherwise.

*

I wanted to teach a language because I wanted to talk to a part of myself that I have forgotten. But I didn't last more than a day on the job, apparently. I wasn't like jelly at my center, but close. I was snow. I was just the snow coming down and I had nothing to give to anyone else today except a cold deafness. I felt unfit to talk about words, which are warm things that connect us. I was disconnected, and lost in the sky on the moon.

*

I feel bad about it as I shuffle in my slippered feet through my rough-looking kitchen. I throw out the trash. I notice we have no more garbage bags. Had I had any money, I would have bought coffee, so how I'm going to afford trash bags, I don't know. Ask one of my roommates, maybe? The orange of the walls looks like spaghetti sauce mixed with vodka. They've really begun selling vodka spaghetti sauce at Superfresh. It's a new flavor of Prego. It's the exact same shade as our walls.

There are both fake plants and real plants in the kitchen. My roommates like plants, real or fake—it doesn't matter to them.

I am lost. I feel like the moon, so out there, in orbit—sinking into the blackness, but held in place by something. I am at a loss to say exactly what is holding me in place, but let it suffice to say that just as the best minds in science also cannot explain gravity in any sensible way, neither can I.